Damian Harvey

Illustrated by Sholto Walker

WAILING ROCK

Ginn

Chapter One
Hindle Cove

It was Dylan’s worst nightmare – eight hours squashed in the car while Mum and Dad argued about which way to go.

"We should have turned down that road," said Mum.

"It’s no good telling me now," said Dad, "we’ve gone past it."

"Well, we’ll just have to turn round," said Mum. "Otherwise we’ll end up at Land’s End."

Dad grumbled as he turned the car round and headed back in the other direction.

"Here it is," said Mum. "Turn here."

"I know," said Dad, as he turned down the lane towards Hindle Cove.

Five minutes later, Dad pulled up outside the holiday cottage in Hindle Cove.

"Here at last," said Dad.

"Why don't you two have a look round while your dad and I unpack the car?" said Mum. "Don't go too far though, it'll be getting dark soon. You'd better save the beach for tomorrow."

Apart from the beach, there wasn't a lot to explore. There was only one road in Hindle Cove and that ended in a slope running down to the sea. Dylan and Megan walked the other way, towards a gift shop they'd seen from the car.

As they walked, they passed a row of neat cottages and a small café. The café had tables and chairs outside, and a little window where you could buy ice creams.

The café was closed but they hoped the gift shop would still be open.

They were in luck. The gift shop was still open. It was full of all the usual gift-shop stuff – buckets and spades, beach balls and cuddly toys. But there were a few things of interest – sets of shark teeth, dried starfish, fossils and polished stones.

A book about pirates caught Dylan's eye. He flicked through it, then took it to the counter to pay. The woman at the counter smiled as she put the book in a bag.

"Pirates, eh! We've got our very own pirate here at Hindle Cove."

"A pirate? Here?" said Dylan. He wasn't sure if the woman was teasing him or not.

"Oh yes," the woman replied. "Captain Jack ... he'll take you on a pirate boat trip to the Wailing Rock. He knows all the old pirate stories. He'll even tell you about the ghost of Cut-Throat Bones."

Chapter Two
A Noise in the Dark

When Dylan and Megan left the shop it seemed much darker outside. It was as if they had been inside for hours, instead of just a few minutes. The sun was setting and swirls of mist were rolling in with the tide. Parts of the beach had almost disappeared beneath the mist.

"Oo-er," said Dylan, "looks spooky doesn't it?"

"Yes," said Megan. "I don't suppose we'll be paddling tonight."

Dylan shivered at the thought of it. "Mum and Dad didn't say anything about a pirate," he said.

"Or a ghost," said Megan.

"What did the lady say the ghost was called?" said Dylan.

"Cut-Throat Bones," said Megan.

In the fading light, Dylan tried to read from his new book.

"I can't see anything about a pirate called Cut-Throat Bones," he said.

As they both walked back towards the cottage, the mist was getting thicker. It was even drifting up onto the road and swirling around their feet.

Megan was concentrating on where she was walking, but Dylan was trying to read about a pirate called Blackbeard.

"Wow!" he said.

"What?" said Megan.

"Some people said that after Blackbeard was killed his headless body carried on fighting," said Dylan.

"Yuk!" said Megan. "That's disgusting."

"Shh!" said Dylan. "What was that?"

Dylan and Megan stood perfectly still ... listening.

"There it is again," said Dylan.

They'd both heard it this time. It sounded like something being dragged along the floor.

It was hard to tell where the sound was coming from. There was nothing on the road and they couldn't see the beach because of the mist.

"It's probably nothing," said Dylan.

"We're nearly at the cottage now ... come on," said Megan.

They were almost there when they heard the sound again. It was coming from the end of the road. There was a grunt and the sound of something being dragged.

"Let's go inside," said Megan.

Dylan agreed, but he didn't move. His eyes were fixed on the end of the road. He was sure he'd seen something move in the mist and the growing darkness.

Yes, there it was again. A dark shape was floating in the mist. It was a shape that Dylan recognised. It looked like a hat. A pirate's hat. The kind that would have been worn by Blackbeard. Or perhaps, by the ghost of Cut-Throat Bones.

"Look!" whispered Dylan. His finger was shaking as he pointed.

Megan was already looking. Her face had gone white and her eyes were like saucers.

"What is it?" asked Megan.

Dylan didn't need to answer. The thing was getting closer and they could both see what it was. It was a hat. A black, three-cornered hat. A pirate's hat.

Megan held Dylan's arm tightly.

"Let's go," she said. "Quick!"

But Dylan couldn't move. He felt as though his legs had turned to jelly.

They heard a grunt and then the dragging, crunching sound came again.

Whatever it was, it was coming up the slope from the beach ... straight towards them.

As they watched, they saw that it wasn't just a hat coming up from the beach. There was a head beneath the hat.

They could see a man's face. He had a patch over one eye, big hoop earrings in his ears, long straggly hair and a big, bushy black beard.

The head stopped. It seemed to look straight at Dylan and Megan. Then it turned and laughed a terrible laugh.

"It's ... it's ... Cut-Throat Bones," cried Dylan.

"And he's not on his own," said Megan.

There was another face floating up from the beach.

Megan gasped. "It looks like ... It's Dad!" said Megan in amazement.

It *was* Dad, and in less than a minute he had walked up from the beach.

"This is Captain Jack," said Dad, introducing the man in the pirate hat.

"Hi kids," said Captain Jack.

The captain didn't seem as creepy now that they could see him properly. Captain Jack was wearing a pirate hat and a sweatshirt that said 'Captain Jack's Pirate Boat Trips' on the front. He also had a bushy black beard and a plastic sword in his belt. His eye patch was now pushed back on his head.

"Your dad was kind enough to help me push my boat up the beach," said the captain. "It's hard work on your own."

"The captain says he'll take us out to the Wailing Rock in the morning," explained Dad.

"You'll have to get up early though," said the captain. "I will only be able to do one trip tomorrow before the tide goes out."

"Aye, aye, Captain," said Dad, saluting. "We'll see you in the morning."

Chapter Three
Captain Jack's Boat Trip

Early next morning, everyone was outside waiting for Captain Jack.

Dylan was reading his book.

Megan was watching a lady painting shells. The lady was sat on a deckchair with a small dog by her feet. Every now and then she threw a stick and the little dog dashed off along the beach to fetch it.

"What's his name?" Megan asked the lady.

"Alfie," she replied. "You can throw the stick for him if you like."

Megan just had time to throw Alfie's stick a few times before Captain Jack arrived. She patted Alfie's head, said goodbye to the lady, and raced off to join the others.

"Ahoy there shipmates," shouted the captain. "Are you ready to set sail?"

"Aye, aye, Captain," said Dad.

Dylan and Megan groaned. Mum shook her head and smiled.

They climbed aboard Captain Jack's boat and were soon bobbing across the waves towards a large rock that stood on its own in the sea.

"That's the Wailing Rock," said Captain Jack.

"Why is it called the Wailing Rock?" asked Megan.

"You'll see," said the captain. "It's special."

They kept their eyes fixed firmly on the rock as the boat got closer.

"Here we are," said Captain Jack.

As the boat made its way round to the far side of the rock, they all saw why it was special. The Wailing Rock looked like a huge white skull. There were two holes near the top that looked like eyes. A piece stuck out like a lumpy nose and, at the bottom, was a wide-open mouth. The waves washed in and out of the mouth, between tooth-like rocks.

"Wow!" said Dylan. "It looks just like a skull!"

Suddenly, a soft moaning sound filled the air …

WooOOooOOoo.

It seemed to come from the mouth of the skull.

"What on earth was that?" said Dad.

"Ahar!" said Captain Jack. "That’s the Wailing Rock."

"How does it do that?" asked Megan, staring at the rock.

"Ahar!" said the captain again. "That's the mystery of it. Some people say it's the wind blowing through the cracks and holes. Others say it's the ghost of old Cut-Throat Bones – the nastiest pirate that ever sailed the seas."

"Huh!" said Dylan. "I've never heard of a pirate called Cut-Throat Bones."

"Of course you haven't," said Captain Jack. "That's because no one ever speaks of him. It's bad luck. Cut-Throat Bones was a nasty pirate, but what happened to him was terrible."

"What happened to him?" said Dylan and Megan together.

"Well!" said Captain Jack. "If you really want to know ... then I'll tell you."

Chapter Four
The Tale of Cut-Throat Bones

"Captain Cut-Throat Bones was the fiercest pirate ever to sail the seas.

He stole more treasure than Captain Kid. He sunk more ships than Blackbeard.

Everyone was afraid of Cut-Throat Bones … even his pirate crew.

Cut-Throat Bones had a hook at the end of his arm and a patch on one eye.

When he was angry he would scrape his hook along one of the ship's cannons. It made a terrible noise. It sounded like fingernails being dragged down a blackboard … but ten times worse.

On one trip, the pirates hadn't eaten for six whole days. Sharks were circling the ship, hoping for a pirate supper.

Cut-Throat Bones stuck his arm in the water and caught one of the sharks with his hook.

In no time at all the pirates were feasting on shark-burgers.

But it was a hard life being a pirate.

The King's navy were after Cut-Throat Bones. One day, there was a terrible sea battle and Cut-Throat Bones' ship was sunk. Cut-Throat Bones jumped into the sea and swam to this rock to hide from the soldiers ... but there was no escape for him. The soldiers were waiting ... and as the tide got higher, Cut-Throat Bones crawled further into the rock. He crawled up towards the eye holes to keep out of the water ... but the tide kept coming in.

The water got deeper and deeper, and the tunnels got narrower and narrower. Cut-Throat Bones found himself stuck as the water rose around him.

For miles around people could hear him wailing for help. People say you could hear the scratching of his hook on the rock as he tried to get away from the rising tide. No one ever saw Cut-Throat Bones again. When the tide went out, all they found was his hat and his hook.

To this very day you can still hear the captain's ghost wailing for help … and sometimes, you can even hear the sound of his hook scratching on the rock."

Chapter Five
Back to the Rock

After the boat trip, Mum and Dad wanted to go into town. Dylan and Megan wanted to spend the day on the beach.

"You can go on the beach when we get back," said Dad. "I promise."

While they were wandering round the shops, Dylan and Megan talked about what they were going to do later. Captain Jack had said you could walk to the Wailing Rock when the tide was out.

"I think we should have a closer look at it," said Dylan.

Megan wasn't so sure.

"Captain Jack said the tide comes in very quickly. He said people often get stuck out there."

"You're not frightened are you?" said Dylan. He made a hook shape with his hand and put on a silly voice.

"WOOOoooOOO," he said. "Captain Cut-Throat Bones is coming for you."

"Don't be daft," said Megan. "Of course I'm not frightened."

It was getting late when they got back to Hindle Cove.

"You promised we could go on the beach," grumbled Dylan.

"I know," said Dad. "You can go for a little while. As long as you don't go out of sight."

Dylan looked out across the beach towards the Wailing Rock.

"No, we won't go out of sight," he said.

It was a long walk to the Wailing Rock – much further than it had seemed in Captain Jack's boat.

"Are you sure this is a good idea?" said Megan. "It's starting to get dark."

"Of course," said Dylan. "We're nearly there now, come on."

The rock looked bigger without the water splashing round it.

It looked creepier too. The setting sun cast strange shadows, making it look even more like a huge skull.

"Let's have a look inside," said Dylan.

Before Megan could say anything, Dylan was climbing over the tooth-like rocks and into the open mouth. She followed him quickly and didn't notice the tide coming in around them.

It was dark inside the cave and their voices echoed off the bare rock.

"This is cool," said Dylan.

"It's freezing," said Megan. "Let's go. I don't like it in here."

"Let's wait and see if it makes that wailing noise," said Dylan, "just once."

"All right ... just once," said Megan, stepping further into the cave. She'd suddenly noticed that she'd been standing in a puddle of water.

Dylan and Megan stood close together and listened. They could hear seagulls crying outside and the sound of the sea in the distance.

Then they heard it. A gust of wind blew through the rock and a soft moaning sound filled the air. WoooOOOoooOOOoooO.

As the creepy wailing sound echoed around them, Dylan and Megan looked at each other.

"Right! We've heard it," said Dylan. "Let's go."

"Ha!" said Megan. "Now who's scared?"

"Not me," said Dylan, stepping back towards the entrance of the cave.

"Urghhhh!" he cried, "what's that?"

Dylan looked down. His foot had disappeared in a pool of water.

"The tide's coming in, Megan," said Dylan. "Look!"

They both looked towards the mouth of the cave. Seawater was pouring in around the tooth-like rocks.

"We'd better get out of here," said Megan. She splashed into the water just behind Dylan. Then it came again … the wailing sound. It was louder this time and took them both by surprise.

"Arghhh!" Dylan and Megan cried out.

"What was that?" asked Megan.

"It's just the wind again," said Dylan.

"No!" said Megan, "there was something else ... listen."

They waited, and the wind moaned through the rock once more. It sent a shiver down Dylan's back. Then he heard another sound. A whining sound that brought him out in goose bumps. It was a sad, lonely sound, like something, or someone, that had been trapped for a long time.

"Hello!" Megan called out. "Is anyone there?"

The whining came again, but this time it was followed by a scratching noise.

"Come on," said Megan. "We have to see what it is."

Dylan stared at her and shook his head. His mouth didn't want to move.

"It's ... it's ... it's Cut-Throat Bones," he said. Dylan could imagine the pirate, stuck in the cave, scraping at the rock with his metal-hooked hand.

Megan climbed higher into the cave and peered into one of the dark tunnels.

"Oh no!" she cried. "It's ..."

"... Alfie – that lady's dog!" said Megan. "He must have climbed up there and got stuck."

Dylan and Megan managed to get Alfie unstuck. He didn't seem to have been hurt and was very glad to see them.

"Come on," said Dylan. "We'd better go before it's too late."

But it was already too late. While they'd been rescuing Alfie, the tide had come in much further. The rocks at the mouth of the cave had been covered and the water was still rising.

Chapter Six
Help!

"What are we going to do?" said Megan. "We can't swim all the way back."

"We'll have to shout for help," said Dylan.

He climbed up towards one of the eyeholes and shouted as loud as he could. "HELP!"

Dylan shouted until his throat hurt and then he climbed down and sat with Megan and Alfie.

The water was still rising, but not as fast as before. Perhaps they wouldn't be drowned after all. Perhaps they'd just have to wait for the tide to go out. That would be bad enough. They'd be in trouble when they got back.

It was getting darker now, and mist was creeping into the cave.

"Look!" said Megan.

Dylan looked. There was a small boat just outside the cave.

"Help!" Dylan shouted.

The boat came slowly into the cave, the oars creaking and splashing. Then it came to a halt in front of the two children.

The boatman smiled kindly at Dylan and Megan. At first they thought it was Captain Jack ... but this man was older. He had the same straggly beard and even wore a patch over one eye.

"You'd better get in," said the man. "This is no place to get stuck at high tide."

The man helped Dylan and Megan into the boat and then rowed silently back to the shore.

While Megan stroked Alfie, Dylan sat and watched the man pulling on the oars. There was a splash as the oars touched the water and a click each time he pulled them back.

At the shore, the boat bumped gently against the sand, and Dylan and Megan clambered out. They were all glad to be back on dry land. Alfie ran off up the road, eager to be home. Dylan and Megan laughed, then turned to say thank you, but the man was already disappearing back into the mist.

"Thank you," shouted Dylan, waving.

The man raised one arm to wave back and Dylan and Megan stared in shock as the hook on the end of his arm glinted in the moonlight.